THE

THE UNOFFICIAL HOGWARTS COCKTAIL BOOK

SPELLBINDING SPRITZES, FANTASTICAL OLD-FASHIONEDS,
MAGICAL MARGARITAS, AND MORE ENCHANTING RECIPES

BERTHA BARMANN

Published by:
Ulysses Press
PO Box 3440
Berkeley, CA 94703
www.ulyssespress.com

ISBN: 978-1-64604-350-7
Library of Congress Control Number: 2022936258

Printed in China
10 9 8 7 6 5 4 3 2 1

Acquisitions editor: Claire Sielaff
Managing editor: Claire Chun
Editor: Michele Anderson
Proofreader: Kate St.Clair
Front cover design: David Hastings
Production: Winnie Liu
Cover artwork: martini glass © AkimD/shutterstock.com
Artwork: photos on pages 26, 64, 72, 80, 102 by Thor's Eye Photography. Remaining images from Shutterstock.com—pages 14–15, Yarrrrrbright; page 17, Hihitetlin; page 18, gresei; page 21, zoomik; page 22, Marina Kaiser; pages 25, 40, 43, 52, 56, 59, 71, 83, 84, 97, Brent Hofacker; page 29, YARUNIV Studio; page 30, Goskova Tatiana; pages 32–33, EyesTravelling; page 35, PavelKant; page 36, Richard Podgurski; page 39, comeirrez; page 44, Kitty Bern; page 47, Kozak_studio; page 48, Mateusz Gzik; page 51, Kolpakova Svetlana; page 55, Maria Bocharova; page 60, Wollertz; page 63, Maksym Fesenko; page 67, Coolnina; page 68, 5PH; page 75, PavelLebedev; page 76, Pixel-Shot; pages 78–79, Andrei Mayatnik; page 87, Gecko Studio; page 88, Wild Drag; page 91, PixHound; pages 92–93, Anna Zheludkova; page 94, Dr Faulkner; page 98, Alexander Prokopenko; page 101, Andrew Pustiakin; page 105, Mateusz Gzik; page 107, Matthew Thomas Nicholson; page 109, Goskova Tatiana; page 111, Oksana.Bondar; page 112, Alp Aksoy; page 115, Andrei Mayatnik; pages 116–17, Maya Kruchankova; page 118, zarzamora; page 121, JLMcAnally; page 122, Alphonsine Sabine; page 125, New Africa; page 126, Eric Ezequiel Irazabal; page 128, Dina Belenko

CONTENTS

INTRODUCTION

What better way to celebrate this beloved series than by raising a toast and sipping on something wonderful? Whether you are a bartending beginner or a seasoned potions master, this book of cocktails will take you on a delightful journey across subjects, seasons, and characters. From magical mocktails to enchantingly boozy beverages, there is something for everyone in these pages. Now dust off your cauldron and let us begin. Cheers!

CHAPTER 1

THE MAGICAL BARTENDER

GLASSWARE

At the foundation of any bar is glassware. After all, how else are you going to show off your incredible potions and elixirs? Glassware comes in tons of different shapes and sizes, some more versatile and some designed to serve a very specific purpose for just one or two kinds of drinks. While the glass does not necessarily make or break a good cocktail, it certainly adds to the experience and can give a great cocktail that magical boost. Below you will find some of the basic and most versatile types of glasses. At minimum, it is best to have a set of wineglasses, rocks glasses, and cocktail or martini glasses in your cupboards or on your bar cart. From there you can build your collection as you experiment with cocktails. A bartender with the right utensils and glassware on hand can serve cocktails that look just as enchanting as they taste.

MUST-HAVE GLASSWARE

CHAMPAGNE FLUTE OR COUPE—flutes are tall, narrow glasses with a curved bowl tapering up to a slightly narrower opening; they are designed to keep bubbles intact by reducing the surface area of the beverage. A coupe is a shorter, squatter stemmed glass. Most cocktails that require bubbly will be served in a flute or coupe.

COCKTAIL GLASS—this is a stemmed glass with a V-shaped bowl and a wide opening. Use a cocktail glass for cocktails that are served "up," that is, shaken or stirred but served without ice.

COLLINS OR HIGHBALL GLASSES—they are often used interchangeably. Both are tall, cylindrical glasses used for drinks over ice that often have a higher percentage of mixers to alcohol. A Collins glass is slightly larger than a highball.

IRISH COFFEE GLASS—this is a small, footed glass mug with a handle and is used for Irish coffees, hot toddies, and other warm punches.

MARTINI GLASS—this is very similar to, and often used interchangeably with, a cocktail glass. However, a true traditional martini glass will have a more acute V and a slightly flared conical shape.

ROCKS (OLD-FASHIONED) GLASS—this is a short, squat glass. Frequently used to serve drinks over ice (or on the rocks) or drinks built in the glass rather than in a cocktail shaker, the glass is designed with a heavy bottom to stand up to muddling (that is, smashing ingredients).

MARGARITA GLASS—this is a shallow-bowled, wide-rimmed glass used mainly for margaritas and other frozen beverages. The shallowness of the glass does not lend itself to safely sipping a fully liquid drink, so reserve this for blended, semi-frozen beverages.

SHOT GLASS—short, squat, and sturdy, this glass holds about 1½ ounces, or just enough to swallow in one gulp. It is also useful in a home bar to serve as a measuring utensil if you do not have a separate jigger.

RED WINE GLASS—this is a stemmed glass with a wider bowl and a narrower top than a white wine glass, which allows the aromas of the wine to collect and funnel toward the drinker's nose.

WHITE WINE GLASS—this is also tall and stemmed, but white wine glasses are narrower than their red wine counterparts and vary less in size from bowl to lip. The smaller shape is meant to help preserve the chill on white wine.

TAKING CARE OF GLASSWARE

Hand-wash the glasses carefully with warm water and mild soap, or with a detergent made specifically for glass. Do not use steel wool or an abrasive sponge—you may risk scratching the glassware. Let the glasses air-dry upside down, or dry them by hand with a lint-free towel to avoid causing water spots. It is not recommended to put glassware in the dishwasher because it might break (unless you have a reliable repair charm at the ready).

YOUR BAR'S FOUNDATION

A wide variety of cocktails call for a wide variety of ingredients, from simple vodka to off-the-beaten-path crème de violette. Since none of us want to be caught snooping around in the potions master's closet for an ingredient we do not have on hand, I have laid out in the following list everything you need.

BREWING BASICS

- Flavored vodkas (orange, vanilla, coffee)
- Gin
- Rum (light, gold, spiced, coconut)
- Tequila
- Triple sec, Cointreau, or other orange liqueur
- Vodka
- Whiskey

EXCEEDING EXPECTATIONS

(all of the above and...):

- Amaretto
- Bourbon
- Brandy (regular, apple, apricot)
- Cachaça
- Cognac
- Mezcal
- Rum (dark)
- Scotch and bourbon

ADVANCED POTION-MAKING MATERIALS

(all of the above and…):

- Absinthe
- Bacardi 151
- Moonshine
- Rye

LIQUEURS AND OTHER SPIRITS

- Anise liqueur (like sambuca or something similar)
- Beer
- Bitters (Angostura, Peychaud's, aromatic)
- Blue curaçao
- Campari or Aperol
- Cherry whiskey
- Cinzano
- Cognac
- Crème de cacao
- Crème de cassis
- Crème de violette
- Drambuie
- Fernet-Branca or other brand of amaro
- Frangelico
- Galliano liqueur
- Ginger beer
- Irish cream
- Kahlúa (or other coffee liqueur)
- Maraschino liqueur
- Peach schnapps
- Peppermint schnapps
- Pimm's No. 1
- Prosecco, Champagne
- Raspberry liqueur (such as Chambord)
- Sake
- Sloe gin
- St-Germain liqueur
- Strawberry liqueur
- Vermouth (dry, extra dry, and sweet; Martini Rosso)
- White crème de menthe

GARNISHES

- Cinnamon sticks
- Citrus (limes, lemons, oranges)
- Eggs
- Fruit (peaches, raspberries, strawberries, blueberries)
- Green olives

- Honey
- Maraschino cherries
- Mint
- Sugar (cubes, sanding sugar)
- Edible luster dust or edible glitter

MIXERS

- Agave nectar
- Blood orange juice
- Cola
- Cranberry juice
- Espresso
- Ginger ale
- Grapefruit juice
- Grenadine
- Orange juice
- Passion fruit juice or nectar
- Pineapple juice
- Rose's lime juice
- Seltzer, club soda, or tonic
- Simple syrup
- Sugarcane syrup

BASIC TOOLS

If you want to make brews and tonics worthy of an "Outstanding" grade on your nasty and exhausting potions test, these tools will give you a leg up.

ABSINTHE SPOON—not too many cocktails call for absinthe, but if you feel like indulging in a dance with the green fairy, you will need an absinthe spoon. It is typically like a trowel and has holes in the middle. You rest the spoon over your glass of absinthe, place a sugar cube on top of the spoon, and pour water over the cube to let the sugar water drip slowly into the glass.

BAR SPOON—this is a teaspoon with an extra-long handle. It is basic but crucial for mixing ingredients in tall glasses.

BLENDER—if you do not have a reliable pulverizing charm on hand, a blender will be your best friend for coladas and other frozen beverages.

COCKTAIL SHAKER—the best ones are metal (to quickly chill drinks), have a tightly fitted top to prevent drips, and include a built-in strainer. Look for one that holds at least 16 ounces so your ingredients have room to mix and combine. In a pinch, you could also opt for a "Boston shaker," which is a glass pint glass with a metal cup fitted on tightly.

CORKSCREW—the patriarch of a certain redheaded wizarding family would no doubt be fascinated by a battery-operated wine opener, but a basic double-hinged wine key works just as well as fancier versions.

DECANTER—it is handy to have one around if you enjoy robust red wines. Pour in the wine and let it sit to open up, soften the tannins, and aerate. You might also want a stoppered decanter to store Scotch whisky or just if it matches your bar cart vibe.

JIGGER—like a wand to a witch or wizard, the jigger is the most crucial of tools for a bartender. While you can use a standard shot glass in a pinch, a jigger is the best way to measure your cocktail ingredients. Usually shaped like an hourglass, this handy tool measures 1 ounce on one end and 1½ ounces on the other. Most cocktails are about the proportions rather than the amount of an ingredient. A jigger will help you precisely portion out your elements.

MIXING GLASS—this is any tall glass big enough to stir (not shake) ingredients in. You can also use this tool as the bottom half of your Boston shaker.

MUDDLER—this is a wooden or plastic masher used to smash (that is, muddle) herbs, citrus, or other ingredients against the bottom of a glass.

PARING KNIFE AND SMALL CUTTING BOARD—these are for cutting citrus for twisting, juicing, or garnishing.

STRAINER—if you go for a Boston shaker instead of a cocktail shaker, you will definitely need a strainer, but it is good to have one on hand either way. A strainer will be crucial for making sure that no extra ice gets into your drink and waters it down.

CHAPTER 2

SEASONAL SPECIALTIES

GOOD OLD-FASHIONED LIQUID LUCK

YIELD: 1 SERVING

½ teaspoon sugar

3 dashes Angostura bitters

1 teaspoon water

2 ounces bourbon

orange peel, for garnish

Sports are a big part of the autumn season, and whether you are watching football or a game played on broomsticks, it cannot hurt to sip on a bit of good old-fashioned luck (even if its results are just a placebo effect).

- To a rocks glass, add sugar, bitters, and water. Stir until the sugar is mostly dissolved.

- Fill the glass with ice cubes, add the bourbon, and stir with a barspoon to combine.

- Express an orange peel over the glass, then drop the peel in, for garnish.

> Tip: *Express* is a bartending term meaning to squeeze a citrus rind so that its oils are brought to the top. It adds a little extra flavor and scent over your cocktail.

RUM SHOOTER OF FIRE

YIELD: 1 SERVING

1 ounce green Chartreuse

1 ounce 151-proof rum

This shot is based on the Flaming Dragon, an appropriate name for a shooter celebrating the brave witches and wizards who put their names into a certain flaming goblet (as well as the one who decidedly did not).

- Mix the green Chartreuse and rum in a shot glass.

- Carefully light the shot on fire.

- Let the flames warm the concoction for about 20 seconds.

- Blow out fire.

- Swallow the shot quickly (take care, as it will be hot).

EGGNOG

6 large egg yolks

½ cup granulated sugar

1 cup heavy whipping cream

2 cups milk

½ teaspoon ground nutmeg

pinch of salt

¼ teaspoon vanilla extract

¼ cup brandy, adding
more to taste (optional)

ground cinnamon,
for garnish

cinnamon sticks, for garnish

Eggnog is a classic Christmas drink in wizarding and nonwizarding worlds alike. A favorite of the Hogwarts groundskeeper, this eggnog recipe (featuring both alcoholic and nonalcoholic options) is sure to boost everyone's holiday spirit.

- Whisk the egg yolks and sugar in a bowl until creamy.

- Over medium-high heat, combine the cream, milk, nutmeg, and salt in a saucepan, stirring often until mixture is just barely simmering.

- Temper the egg mixture by adding a spoonful of the hot milk mixture and whisking. Repeat, adding 1 spoonful at a time.

- Once the eggs have been thoroughly tempered (you may have added most or all of the hot milk mixture to the eggs), pour everything back into the saucepan.

- Whisk continuously over medium heat until the mixture is just slightly thickened (or until it reaches about 160°F).

- Remove from the heat and stir in the vanilla. Stir in the alcohol, if using. Start with ¼ cup brandy and add more to taste if desired. Keep in mind that the mixture will thicken more as it cools.

- Pour the eggnog through a fine-mesh strainer into a pitcher and cover it with plastic wrap.

- Refrigerate until chilled.

- Serve with a sprinkle of cinnamon and a cinnamon stick.

- Store in the fridge for up to 1 week.

Substitutions: Switch out the brandy with rum, whiskey, or bourbon, using the same measurements.

Tip: For a smoother, thinner consistency, add the chilled eggnog to a blender with 1 to 2 tablespoons of milk and blend.

CHRISTMAS PARTY PUNCH

YIELD: 8 SERVINGS

8 cups sparkling wine, around 3 (750-milliliter) bottles of prosecco

1½ cups pomegranate juice

¼ cup sugar

2 oranges sliced thinly (discard the end pieces)

½ cup pomegranate seeds

fresh rosemary sprigs, for garnish (optional)

This punch recipe is inspired by the one served at the potions master's holiday party. While the results are not a deep purple, the pomegranate juice does turn the punch a wonderful, Christmasy red!

- In a large punch bowl or pitcher, mix the sparkling wine with the pomegranate juice and sugar. Stir until the sugar dissolves.

- Add the orange slices and pomegranate seeds. Mix again.

- Right before serving, add 4 cups of ice.

- Serve in a punch glass or rocks glass and garnish with a rosemary spring, if using.

> Tip: To make the punch less sweet, add only 1 tablespoon of sugar.

SPRING HOLIDAY GIMLET

YIELD: 1 SERVING

2 ounces gin

1 ounce St-Germain

1 ounce lime juice

1 lime, thinly sliced, for garnish

While the Easter holidays are not necessarily a favorite of the students at Hogwarts (mostly due to the amount of homework assigned by professors), it is still a time of awakening. Plus, you can always find something to raise a glass to, even if you are just celebrating finishing your History of Magic homework.

⟩ Add the gin, St-Germain, and lime juice to a shaker with ice and shake until chilled.

⟩ Strain into a coupe glass with ice.

⟩ Add a thin slice of lime for garnish.

VALENTINE'S LOVE POTION

YIELD: 1 SERVING

2 ounces gin

½ ounce orange liqueur or triple sec

½ ounce freshly squeezed lemon juice

1 egg white

pinch of edible pearl white luster dust (optional)

sliced lemon, for garnish

Inspired by the mother-of-pearl sheen on the wizarding world's most potent love potion, this recipe takes the classic White Lady cocktail and makes it all the more bewitching with a sprinkle of luster dust.

- To a cocktail shaker add the gin, orange liqueur, lemon juice, egg white, and luster dust (if using) and dry shake.

- Add ice and shake until chilled.

- Strain into a chilled cocktail or coupe glass. Add lemon for garnish.

> Tip: "Dry shake" is a bartending term meaning to shake a cocktail without ice.

BOOZY KNICKERBOCKER GLORY

YIELD: 1 SERVING

1 (24-ounce) bottle strawberry or chocolate syrup

3 ounces gin (or more to taste)

1 can strawberry pie filling

1 tub vanilla ice cream

1 quart fresh strawberries

1 quart fresh raspberries

1 tub either raspberry or strawberry ice cream

whipped cream, for garnish (optional)

sprig of fresh mint, for garnish (optional)

ice cream wafer or wafer rolls, for garnish (optional)

chopped nuts, for garnish (optional)

maraschino cherry, for garnish (optional)

This is the perfect dessert for someone who is a little upset about getting 36 presents instead of 37. This boozy spin on the Knickerbocker Glory ice cream sundae uses gin, but feel free to replace it with a flavored vodka or other liquor of your choice.

- In a tall sundae glass, pour in some strawberry or chocolate syrup and add a splash of gin. Add a tablespoon of strawberry pie filling. Add a scoop of vanilla ice cream.

- Add a layer of fresh strawberries and fresh raspberries.

- Add another tablespoon of strawberry pie filling.

- Pour in another splash of gin.

- Add a scoop of the raspberry or strawberry ice cream.

- Repeat the layers until the glass is full, being sure to alternate between the fruit-flavored ice cream and vanilla ice cream.

- Garnish the dessert with any other toppings of your choice, if using, like whipped cream, fresh fruit, a sprig of mint, wafer, chopped nuts, and a maraschino cherry.

STRAWBERRY MARGARITA

YIELD: 4 SERVINGS

6 ounces tequila

2 ounces triple sec

8 ounces frozen sliced strawberries in syrup

4 ounces frozen limeade concentrate

fresh strawberries, for garnish

Inspired by what the trio had for dessert at the '94 World Cup, this recipe adds strawberry to the classic margarita, perfect to enjoy on warm summer nights with friends and family.

- Fill a blender with ice and crush the ice.

- Add in the tequila, triple sec, strawberries, and limeade. Blend the mixture for 30 seconds or until smooth.

- Serve the cocktail in margarita glasses with a sliced fresh strawberry for garnish.

CHAPTER 3

PLACES

SPIKED PUMPKIN JUICE PUNCH

YIELD: 6 SERVINGS

4 cups apple cider or apple juice

1½ cups peach nectar

1 cup pumpkin puree

1 cup spiced rum

¼ teaspoon ground cinnamon

¼ teaspoon ground nutmeg

¼ teaspoon pumpkin pie spice

2 bottles Champagne or sparkling wine, chilled

star anise, for garnish (optional)

sliced oranges and apples, for garnish (optional)

A beloved classic, pumpkin juice is served with nearly every meal at the castle, as well as on the scarlet steam engine. This spiked recipe is best served well chilled.

- In a large punch bowl, whisk together the apple cider or juice, peach nectar, pumpkin puree, rum, cinnamon, nutmeg, and pumpkin pie spice until the mixture is well combined.

- Pour the Champagne or sparkling wine into the bowl and stir.

- Garnish the punch with star anise, and orange and apple slices, if using.

- Serve the punch immediately.

FORBIDDEN FOREST FIZZ

YIELD: 1 SERVING

2 parts Champagne
or sparkling wine

1 part orange juice

If you are going to go gallivanting into the forest, you might want some liquid courage. This effervescent cocktail inspired by the Buck's Fizz will lighten the mood even when you are in the forest for detention or are following a trail of spiders.

⌣ Pour the ingredients into a Champagne flute and enjoy.

EXPLODING LEMON GIN FIZZ

YIELD: 1 SERVING

1½ ounces gin

2 ounces freshly squeezed lemon juice

simple syrup, to taste

club soda

lemon and lime slices, for garnish

fresh mint, for garnish

Inspired by a drink served at the wizarding pub in London, this lemony cocktail is, thankfully, not hazardous to the drinker's health (unless, of course, it is consumed in great quantities, so please drink responsibly).

- Fill a rocks glass with ice.
- Pour in the gin and fresh lemon juice.
- Top it off with simple syrup and club soda.
- Garnish the cocktail with lemon and lime slices and fresh mint.

Tip: To make quick and easy simple syrup, combine equal parts sugar and water in a saucepan over medium heat. Stir until the sugar is dissolved, then remove from heat. After completely cool, store in an airtight container in the fridge for around one month.

FIRE-INFUSED WHISKEY SHOTS

YIELD: 4 SERVINGS

250 milliliters whiskey (about 1 (8-ounce) bottle)

2 cinnamon sticks

⅛ cup brown sugar

1 teaspoon Tabasco sauce

Another recipe inspired by the pub that serves as the entrance to a certain magical alley (but found all throughout the wizarding world), this spicy whiskey shot is sure to have you and your friends feeling the burn, thanks to the hit of Tabasco. It takes several days to infuse the cinnamon flavor into the whiskey, so be sure to plan ahead.

- Combine the whiskey, cinnamon, and brown sugar in a closed container.

- Age the mixture for 4 to 7 days in a dark, cool place.

- When ready to serve, pour the mixture into shot glasses and add ¼ teaspoon of Tabasco sauce per shot. Let the shots stand for 2 minutes before drinking.

BUTTERSCOTCH BEER

YIELD: 1 SERVING

6 ounces cream soda

1 ounce vanilla vodka

1 ounce butterscotch
schnapps

1 to 2 dashes butter extract

GARNISH
¼ cup heavy
whipping cream

1 tablespoon
powdered sugar

½ ounce Amaretto

There are many recipes out there for nonmagical folk wanting to re-create this wizarding world favorite. This is a chilled version featuring a sweet, whipped topping that has an added kick from Amaretto. The key ingredient is butter extract, which is important to achieve that buttery taste.

- In a beer mug, combine the cream soda, vanilla vodka, butterscotch schnapps, and butter extract and mix thoroughly.

- For the garnish, put the whipping cream in a medium bowl and beat with a mixer until soft peaks form.

- Add the powdered sugar and Amaretto, and continue beating the mixture until stiff peaks form.

- Place a heaping spoonful of the cream on top of the drink for garnish.

GILL-GROWING WEED WATER

YIELD: 1 SERVING

juice of ½ lime

½ small cucumber skinned and chopped

2 slices lemon

½ teaspoon honey

1½ ounces alcohol of your choice, like gin or vodka

8 ounces sparkling mineral water, chilled

sliced lime, for garnish

fresh mint, for garnish

fresh elderflowers, for garnish (optional)

This refreshing cocktail will not help you grow gills and breathe underwater, but it is inspired by the magical plant that does.

- Prepare the fresh ingredients by halving a lime, juicing one half and slicing the other, skinning and chopping half of a small cucumber, and slicing a lemon.

- Once ingredients are prepared, add cucumber, lemon, and honey to a cocktail shaker. Muddle.

- Add lime juice, alcohol of your choice, and some ice to the cocktail shaker. Cover and shake until well chilled.

- To a large wine glass, add 3 to 4 ice cubes and mineral water. Strain the mixture from the cocktail shaker into the glass and stir to combine.

- Garnish with lime slices, a sprig of fresh mint, and elderflowers, if using.

> Note: This cocktail can easily turn into an equally refreshing mocktail; just forgo the alcohol entirely!

For all the courageous lionhearts out there, the following cocktails are all inspired by the house colors of red and gold. Whip up one or two to celebrate a brave deed, or make up a whole tray of them to impress party guests.

HOUSE OF LIONS

LIONHEART KIR ROYALE

YIELD: 1 SERVING

½ ounce crème de cassis

dry Champagne (or other sparkling wine), to top

lemon twist or orange peel, for garnish

◗ Pour the crème de cassis into a Champagne flute and top it with the Champagne.

◗ Garnish it with a lemon twist or orange peel.

NEARLY HEADLESS NEGRONI

YIELD: 1 SERVING

1 ounce gin

1 ounce Campari

1 ounce sweet vermouth

orange peel, for garnish

- Add the gin, Campari, and sweet vermouth to a cocktail shaker with ice and shake until the drink is well chilled.

- Strain it into a rocks glass filled with ice.

- Garnish it with an orange peel.

FORTUNA MAJOR
MARTINI

YIELD: 1 SERVING

1½ ounces vodka

½ ounce orange liqueur

½ ounce dry vermouth

½ ounce cranberry juice

fresh cranberries, for
garnish (optional)

- Combine the vodka, orange liqueur, vermouth,
cranberry juice, and ice in a cocktail shaker. Shake
vigorously to chill the cocktail.

- Pour it into a cocktail glass, and serve. Garnish
with fresh cranberries on a cocktail skewer, if using.

FAIRY LIGHT FRENCH 75

YIELD: 1 SERVING

1 ounce gin

½ ounce freshly squeezed lemon juice

½ ounce simple syrup

3 ounces Champagne (or other sparkling wine)

lemon twist, for garnish

To a cocktail shaker with ice, add the gin, lemon juice, and simple syrup. Shake well, then strain into a Champagne flute.

Top it with the Champagne.

Garnish it with a lemon twist.

The following cocktails are all in shades of yellow and black to celebrate hardworking, patient, and loyal students of this house.

HOUSE OF
BADGERS

BADGER WHAMMER

YIELD: 1 SERVING

1½ ounces banana liqueur

1 ounce peach schnapps

pineapple juice

sliced banana, for garnish (optional)

fresh mint leaves, for garnish (optional)

- Fill a highball glass with ice.

- Add the banana liqueur and peach schnapps to the glass.

- Top with the pineapple juice and stir until the ingredients are combined.

- Garnish it with the sliced banana and mint leaves, if using.

FRIAR'S FIZZ

1½ ounces citrus vodka
(Ketel One Citroen)

¾ ounce lemon juice

½ ounce simple syrup

club soda

lemon wedge, for garnish

Fill a highball glass with ice. Add the citrus vodka, lemon juice, and simple syrup, and stir.

Top it with club soda and garnish it with a lemon wedge.

SPROUT'S SIDECAR

YIELD: 1 SERVING

sugar rim (optional)

1½ ounces cognac

¾ ounce orange liqueur

¾ ounce freshly
squeezed lemon juice

pinch of edible
yellow luster dust

orange twist, for garnish

Wet the rim of a coupe glass and dip in sugar to create a sugar rim, if desired.

Add the cognac, orange liqueur, lemon juice, and yellow luster dust to a shaker with ice. Shake the mixture until it is well chilled.

Strain the drink into the prepared coupe glass and garnish it with an orange twist.

BLACK MARTINI

YIELD: 1 SERVING

1 part black
raspberry liqueur

1 part vodka

lemon twist, for garnish

Put the ice, raspberry liqueur, and vodka into a cocktail shaker and shake vigorously.

Strain it into a cocktail glass and garnish with a lemon twist.

Note: If you want your Black Martini even darker, simply add 1 drop each of red, green, and blue food coloring to the cocktail shaker with the other ingredients. Feel free to adjust the amounts until the potion color is to your liking.

For those who value wit, creativity, and originality, this next section of blue- and bronze-colored cocktails will surely spark your fancy.

HOUSE OF EAGLES

SAPPHIRE DIADEM MARTINI

YIELD: 1 SERVING

¾ ounce Hendrick's gin

¾ ounce crème de violette

¼ ounce blue curaçao

¼ ounce freshly squeezed lemon juice

3 ounces Champagne, chilled

star anise, for garnish

To a pint glass with ice, add the gin, crème de violette, blue curaçao, and lemon juice and stir until chilled.

Strain the cocktail into a coupe glass, and top it with the Champagne. Garnish with star anise.

STARRY NIGHT IN THE TOWER

YIELD: 1 SERVING

MILKY WAY ICE
2 cups hot water
10 butterfly pea flowers

STARRY NIGHT COCKTAIL
crushed ice
2 ounces vodka
½ ounce freshly squeezed lime juice
4 to 6 ounces ginger beer
crushed Milky Way Ice

MILKY WAY ICE

- In a small saucepan, bring water to a boil. Turn off the heat and add the butterfly pea flowers.

- Allow the tea to steep for 3 to 4 minutes.

- Strain out flowers and let cool.

- Pour the cooled mixture into ice cube trays and freeze.

STARRY NIGHT IN THE TOWER COCKTAIL

- Partially fill a glass with crushed clear ice.

- Top with the crushed Milky Way Ice.

- Add the vodka, lime juice, and ginger beer.

- Top it with additional Milky Way Ice.

BRONZE EAGLE

YIELD: 1 SERVING

1½ ounces amber vermouth

2 ounces fino sherry

orange bitters

pinch of edible
bronze luster dust

lemon peel, for garnish

⌣ Fill a cocktail shaker with ice and pour in the vermouth, fino sherry, a few drops of orange bitters, and a pinch of edible bronze luster dust. Stir the mixture with a bar spoon until it is well chilled.

⌣ Strain the cocktail into a coupe and garnish it with a lemon peel.

BRONZE SAZERAC

YIELD: 1 SERVING

absinthe, to rinse

1 sugar cube

½ teaspoon cold water

3 dashes Peychaud's bitters

2 dashes Angostura bitters

1¼ ounces rye whiskey

1¼ ounces cognac

lemon peel or twist,
for garnish

- Rinse a chilled rocks glass with absinthe. Set aside after discarding any excess absinthe.

- Muddle the sugar cube, water, and Peychaud's and Angostura bitters in a cocktail shaker.

- Add the rye, cognac, and ice. Stir until well chilled.

- Put the lid on the shaker and strain the drink into the prepared glass.

- Express a lemon peel over the drink, then garnish it with the peel.

Now it is time to honor the resourceful, cunning, and ambitious
students with a host of green and silver beverages.

HOUSE OF SNAKES

SALAZAR SOUR

YIELD: 1 SERVING

1 ounce Midori

1 ounce vodka

½ ounce freshly
squeezed lemon juice

½ ounce freshly
squeezed lime juice

club soda, to top

maraschino cherry,
for garnish

- Add the Midori, vodka, and lemon and lime juices to a rocks glass with ice.

- Stir the mixture to combine, then top it with the club soda.

- Garnish it with a maraschino cherry.

SNAKEBITE SHOT

YIELD: 1 SERVING

2 ounces whiskey

splash to ½ ounce lime
cordial, or to taste

Pour the whiskey and lime cordial into a cocktail
shaker with ice. Shake it until the drink is chilled.

Strain the drink into a shot glass. Bottoms up!

DEATH IN THE AFTERNOON

YIELD: 1 SERVING

1½ ounces absinthe

4½ ounces chilled Champagne

◐ Pour the absinthe into a coupe.

◐ Top it with the Champagne.

SANCTIMONIA VINCET SEMPER MARTINI

YIELD: 1 SERVING

1 cucumber

½ ounce dry vermouth

3 ounces gin

pinch of edible
silver luster dust

- Cut the cucumber in half. Use a vegetable peeler to peel 1 of the halves of the cucumber.

- Cut the peeled half of the cucumber into slices; you will need 4 to 6 slices for the cocktail. Add the cucumber slices to a pint glass.

- Pour the vermouth into the pint glass and muddle the cucumbers.

- Transfer muddled cucumbers and vermouth to a cocktail shaker with ice. Add the gin and edible luster dust.

- Shake until the mixture is chilled, then strain it into a martini glass.

- Garnish the drink using a slice of the unpeeled cucumber on a cocktail skewer.

> Substitutions: Feel free to use vodka
> instead of gin!

CHAPTER 4

PEOPLE

GOLDEN POPTAILS

YIELD: 4 SERVINGS

POPSICLES
½ cup lemon juice
½ cup sugar
1¾ cups cold water
1 teaspoon edible
gold luster dust

**GOLDEN POPTAIL
COCKTAIL**
lemon popsicles
1 bottle chilled prosecco
or Champagne

The hard-to-spot, flying golden ball that can win the game takes a frozen form in this easy-to-make, bubbly cocktail.

POPSICLES

- For the popsicles, whisk together the lemon juice and sugar in a bowl until the sugar has completely dissolved into a syrup.

- Add the syrup to the cold water and mix thoroughly.

- Add the edible gold luster dust to the liquid and stir it to combine.

- Pour the liquid into round ice molds. You want the popsicles to be spherical.

- Freeze them overnight.

GOLDEN POPTAIL COCKTAIL

- When you are ready to make the cocktails, allow the popsicles to sit at room temperature for 5 minutes and then take them out of the molds.

- Put 1 popsicle each into rocks glasses and top each drink with the prosecco or Champagne.

- Place any extra popsicles in a plastic bag and store them in the freezer.

HEADMASTER'S LEMON DROP

YIELD: 1 SERVING

sugar rim (optional)

2 ounces vodka

½ ounce triple sec

1 ounce freshly
squeezed lemon juice

1 ounce simple syrup

lemon twist, for garnish

One of the headmaster's favorite treats was sherbet lemon hard candy. This lemon drop martini has the same flavor profile: a perfect mix of sweet and citrusy.

) Wet the rim of a cocktail glass and dip in sugar to create a sugar rim, if desired.

) To a cocktail shaker with ice, add the vodka, triple sec, lemon juice, and simple syrup and shake until chilled.

) Strain the cocktail into the sugar-rimmed glass and garnish it with a lemon twist.

MARAUDERS' MARGARITA

YIELD: 2 SERVINGS

SPICY LIME SALT
½ cup kosher salt
or flaky sea salt

2 tablespoons lime zest,
from fresh limes

1 tablespoon chili powder

**MARAUDERS'
MARGARITA**
4 ounces tequila

2 ounces triple sec

3 limes, juiced and divided

1 tablespoon agave nectar

1 jalapeño pepper

lime wedges, for garnish

This crowd-pleasing classic with a spicy spin is so satisfyingly boozy that it will have anyone up to no good after a few rounds. Just make sure to stay out of a snively someone's way or you might get in trouble...

SPICY LIME SALT

- Make the Spicy Lime Salt by combining the salt, lime zest, and chili powder in a small bowl.

- Pour the Spicy Lime Salt onto a plate. Use the juice from 1 lime to wet the rims of 2 margarita or rocks glasses. Dip the rims into the salt.

MARAUDERS' MARGARITA

- For the margarita, fill the glasses with ice, and set them aside.

- Halve the jalapeño and deseed. Reserve one half for garnish, dice the other half.

- Pour the tequila, triple sec, lime juice from 2 limes, agave nectar, and diced jalapeño into a cocktail shaker over ice. Cover, and vigorously shake the mixture until it is well chilled.

- Strain the drink into the prepared glasses, and garnish each one with the jalapeño slices and lime wedges.

UNICORN BLOOD

YIELD: 1 SERVING

2 ounces gin

½ ounce maraschino liqueur

¼ ounce crème de violette

¾ ounce freshly squeezed lemon juice

dash of silver edible luster dust

This is a shimmery take on the Aviation cocktail, that, fortunately, will not curse you to live a half-life when you drink it.

- To a cocktail shaker with ice, add the gin, maraschino liqueur, crème de violette, lemon juice, and silver luster dust and shake until chilled.
- Strain the drink into a cocktail glass.

BERRY WINE
SANGRIA

YIELD: 1 SERVING

1 (750 milliliter) bottle chilled mild red wine (such as lambrusco)

1 cup sliced strawberries

1 cup raspberries

1 cup blueberries

1 cup blackberries

¾ cup brandy

2 cups lemon-lime soda

This berry sangria is inspired by the thousand-year-old, house-elf-made berry wine sold in various magical pubs. Hogwarts' groundskeeper drowned his sorrows in it after his arachnid friend passed away. This sangria version has a sweet, deep flavor and a little bit of fizz, thanks to the lemon-lime soda.

In a large punch bowl or pitcher, mix the wine, strawberries, raspberries, blueberries, blackberries, and brandy. Refrigerate the mixture for at least 1 hour.

Stir the lemon-lime soda into the bowl or pitcher after the wine mixture is well chilled.

Serve the sangria immediately.

MAD-EYE MARTINI

YIELD: 2 SERVINGS

6 ounces vodka

4 ounces lychee juice

splash vermouth

4 brandied cherries,
for garnish

4 lychee, for garnish

The garnish in this lychee martini is inspired by the magical eye of the most famous Auror of all time and member of the Order.

⟩ To a cocktail shaker with ice, add the vodka, lychee juice, and vermouth and shake until it is chilled. Strain the cocktail into 2 martini glasses.

⟩ For the garnish, push a brandied cherry into the center of the lychee and add two of them on a skewer to the drink.

CHAPTER 5

SUBJECTS

EARL GREY TEA COCKTAIL

This tea-based cocktail will have you feeling practically clairvoyant. Luckily, you will not be seeing the Grim in the bottom of your cup, as this recipe does not use loose-leaf tea.

YIELD: AROUND 3 SERVINGS OR 1 (32-OUNCE) TEAPOT

HONEY SIMPLE SYRUP
5 cups water
1 cup honey

EARL GRAY TEA COCKTAIL
2¾ to 3 cups cold Earl Grey tea
4 ounces gin
4 ounces Honey Simple Syrup
1 ounce freshly squeezed lemon juice,
lemon slices, for garnish

HONEY SIMPLE SYRUP

Make the Honey Simple Syrup by bringing 5 cups of water and 1 cup of honey to a simmer and stirring until the honey has dissolved. Store the syrup in the refrigerator in an airtight container.

EARL GREY TEA COCKTAIL

Brew 2¾ to 3 cups of Earl Grey tea following instructions on the tea bag. Store it in the refrigerator to keep it cold.

Add the chilled tea, gin, chilled Honey Simple Syrup, and lemon juice to a 32-ounce teapot. Stir the mixture until the ingredients are combined.

Serve the cocktail in teacups with lemon slices as a garnish.

THE DANCING CUPCAKE

YIELD: 1 SERVING

1 packet red Pop Rocks candy (optional)

2 ounces vodka

1 ounce grenadine

4 ounces lemon-lime soda

maraschino cherries, for garnish (optional)

A cherry soda is one of the Charm's professor's go-to beverages. This take on the Shirley Temple adds booze for an extra kick as well as an optional Pop Rocks rim. It is a pick-me-up almost as good as the charmed cupcakes the good professor uses to cheer up his students.

- Pour the Pop Rocks candy onto a small plate. Wet the rim of a highball glass and dip it into the candy.

- Fill the glass with ice, then add the vodka and grenadine. Top the drink with the soda, then garnish it with a maraschino cherry.

WINGARDIUM MIMOSA

YIELD: 6 GLASSES

⅓ medium seedless watermelon, chilled

1 bottle pink prosecco or rosé Champagne, chilled

This light-as-a-feather mimosa is inspired by the brightest witch of her age's iconic pronunciation instruction. It is "mim-OH-sah" not "mim-oh-SAH!"

- Remove all the black seeds from the watermelon if you find any. Then, scoop the watermelon into a blender.

- Blend the watermelon until it is smooth. Strain through a fine-mesh strainer into a bowl or liquid measuring cup and discard the solids.

- Fill each Champagne flute halfway with the prosecco or Champagne.

- Fill the rest of each glass with the watermelon juice, leaving about an inch of room at the top.

CHOCOLATE MARTINI

YIELD: 1 SERVING

1½ tablespoons
chocolate syrup

2 ounces Baileys
Irish Cream

2 ounces chocolate liqueur

4 ounces vodka

shaved milk or
dark chocolate, for
garnish (optional)

It is well known that it is best to have chocolate on hand when dealing with hooded creatures that can suck out your soul. This Chocolate Martini is sure to bring the warm fuzzies back when it feels like all hope is lost.

⟩ Drizzle the chocolate syrup inside the martini glass.

⟩ Add the Baileys, chocolate liqueur, and vodka to a cocktail shaker filled with ice. Shake the mixture until it is well chilled.

⟩ Strain the drink into the martini glass. Garnish it with shaved chocolate, if using.

EUPHORIC FIG ELIXIR

YIELD: 1 SERVING

FIGGY SAGE SIMPLE SYRUP
1 cup dried figs, sliced

8 fresh sage leaves

1 cup white sugar

1 cup water

EUPHORIC FIG ELIXIR
2 ounces white rum

1 ounce orange liqueur, like Grand Marnier

1 ounce Figgy Sage Simple Syrup

¾ ounce freshly squeezed lemon juice

chilled club soda for topping

sliced fresh figs, for garnish

Inspired by the magical fig found in the first years' herbology textbook (and used in a certain euphoria-inducing potion), this deliciously flavorful and slightly bubbly elixir will have the drinker feeling on top of the world!

FIGGY SAGE SIMPLE SYRUP

- For the Figgy Sage Simple Syrup, in a small saucepan, combine the figs, sage, sugar, and water. Over medium-high heat, bring the mixture to a simmer.

- Stir the mixture to dissolve the sugar.

- Once the sugar dissolves, turn off heat and steep the mixture for at least 30 minutes.

- Strain and store the syrup in the refrigerator in a mason jar or other airtight container.

EUPHORIC FIG ELIXIR COCKTAIL

- For the cocktail, add the rum, orange liqueur, Figgy Sage Simple Syrup, lemon juice, and ice to a cocktail shaker and shake until well chilled.

- Strain the cocktail into an ice-filled glass.

- Top the drink with club soda. Garnish it with sliced fresh figs.

ESPRESSO MARTINI

YIELD: 1 SERVING

2 ounces vodka

½ ounce coffee liqueur,
such as Kahlúa

1 ounce freshly
brewed espresso

½ ounce simple syrup

coffee beans, for garnish

You will need all the help you can get staying awake during a lecture about troll wars. Give yourself a boost with a delicious Espresso Martini.

⌣ To a cocktail shaker with ice, add the vodka, coffee liqueur, espresso, and simple syrup and shake the mixture until it is well chilled.

⌣ Strain the martini into a chilled cocktail glass.

⌣ Garnish it with 3 coffee beans.

POLY POTION

1½ ounces vodka

1 ounce raspberry liqueur, like Chambord

½ ounce unsweetened cranberry juice (do not use cranberry juice cocktail)

½ ounce freshly squeezed lemon juice

½ ounce grenadine

1 small dry-ice cube (optional)

orange peel, for garnish (optional)

We all know this potion can taste pretty nasty if you are using the hair of someone unsavory. But since the cocktails in this book are meant to be enjoyed, we will pretend that the hair of a wonderful person is being used here. Dry ice at the end adds the perfect, and impressive, finishing touch.

- Add the vodka, raspberry liqueur, unsweetened cranberry juice, lemon juice, and grenadine to a cocktail shaker with regular ice cubes.

- Shake the mixture until it is well chilled and then strain the drink into a rocks glass.

- Using tongs (never touch dry ice with your bare hands), add a chunk of dry ice around 1 inch in size to the glass. Garnish with an orange peel, if using.

- Allow everyone to admire your potion-making prowess, but do not drink the dry ice! Wait until the cube disappears before enjoying the cocktail, around 5 minutes.

Tips: Dry ice is available at most grocery stores and sold in large blocks. Buy the dry ice 1 to 2 hours before you plan to serve the cocktail because dry ice does not last in the freezer. Store the plastic bag of dry ice in a cooler with the top off, away from little ones and animal familiars. Right before serving, drop the plastic bag on the ground to make large chunks of dry ice. Then, wearing eye protection and gloves (we do not want this to end with a trip to St. Mungo's!), break the ice into small chunks with an awl, screwdriver, or pick. You want ½-inch to 1-inch chunks. Wrap the chunks in a towel and place them in the cooler with the top off until serving. Remember: no freezer!

LIVING DEAD DRAUGHT

LILAC SIMPLE SYRUP

1 cup water

1 cup sugar

1 cup fresh lilac flowers
(washed and separated
from stems)

3 to 4 drops purple
food coloring (or equal
parts red and blue)

**LIVING DEAD
DRAUGHT COCKTAIL**

2 ounces gin

1 ounces freshly
squeezed lemon juice

1 ounces lilac syrup

1 large egg white

This dreamy lilac cocktail is inspired by the very difficult brew taught to sixth-years in the advanced potions class. The pale lilac color meant that the potion had successfully made it to the halfway stage.

LILAC SIMPLE SYRUP

- For the Lilac Simple Syrup, add the water, sugar, and lilac flowers to a small saucepan on the stove. On medium-high heat, bring the mixture to a boil and stir continuously until the sugar has dissolved.

- Remove the pan from the heat and let cool. Once completely cool, strain the mixture into a mason jar or other airtight container.

- Add the food coloring. Refrigerate, as it's best to have the syrup well chilled before making the cocktail. It will keep for up to 3 weeks in the fridge.

LIVING DEAD DRAUGHT COCKTAIL

- For the cocktail, add the gin, lemon juice, Lilac Simple Syrup, and egg white to a cocktail shaker and dry shake until foamy.

- Add ice to the shaker and shake it again until well chilled.

- Strain the cocktail through a fine-mesh strainer into a coupe or cocktail glass.

BABBLING ICED TEA

YIELD: 1 SERVING

¾ ounce vodka

¾ ounce white rum

¾ ounce silver tequila

¾ ounce gin

¾ ounce triple sec

¾ ounce simple syrup

¾ freshly squeezed ounce lemon juice

cola, to top

lemon slice, for garnish

fresh mint, for garnish

A Long Island Iced Tea can get anyone talking. Drink up and prepare to get chatty!

- Add the vodka, rum, tequila, gin, triple sec, simple syrup, and lemon juice to an ice-filled Collins glass or a pint glass.

- Top the mixture with a splash of the cola and stir.

- Garnish the drink with a lemon slice and fresh mint.

KUMQUAT MOJITO

YIELD: 1 SERVING

20 kumquats (½ pound), halved lengthwise

1 cup mint leaves

1 (10-ounce) bottle calamansi puree

1¾ cups white rum

1 quart club soda

1 large lime, cut into 10 thin wedges

fresh mint, for garnish (optional)

Inspired by a certain spell that transfigures the victim's ears into kumquats, this tasty Kumquat Mojito is far more enjoyable than the spell itself. It is refreshing, unique, and so delicious that you will want to drink the whole pitcher.

- In a large pitcher, combine the halved kumquats and mint leaves. Using a large wooden spoon, vigorously muddle the mixture.

- Pour in the calamansi puree, rum, and club soda and squeeze in the lime wedges.

- Fill the pitcher with ice and serve. Garnish with fresh mint, if using.

> Substitutions: If you can't find calamansi puree, substitute with a 10-ounce can of frozen orange juice concentrate, thawed.

WINGED HORSE'S NECK

YIELD: 1 SERVING

2 ounces bourbon, brandy, or rye whiskey

ginger ale, chilled, to top

lemon peel, for garnish

fresh mint, for garnish

The winged horses at a certain French magic school are said to drink only single malt whiskey. This take on the classic Horse's Neck cocktail uses that preferred liquor, but it makes the cocktail a bit more refreshing for human consumption with ginger ale and a lemon peel garnish.

Pour the liquor into a Collins glass over ice and top it with ginger ale. Garnish the drink with a lemon peel and a sprig of fresh mint.

CHAPTER 6

MOCKTAILS

ENTRANCING ENCHANTMENT LEMONADE

YIELD: 10 SERVINGS

MILKY WAY ICE
(see page 65 for
ingredients and recipe)

LEMONADE
1¾ cups white sugar

8 cups water, divided

1½ cups freshly squeezed
lemon juice, with pulp

lemon slices

Pour the lemonade over the Milky Way Ice and you will see an enchanting purple color develop, which is similar to the color that results when an entrancing enchantment charm is cast.

- Make a batch of Milky Way Ice, following the instructions on page 65.

- For the lemonade, make a simple syrup by combining the sugar and 1 cup of the water in a small saucepan. Stir the mixture to dissolve the sugar as the mixture comes to a boil.

- Remove the syrup from the heat and set it aside to cool.

- Fill a pitcher with ice. Pour the cooled syrup into the pitcher, then stir in the lemon juice, remaining 7 cups water, and lemon slices.

- When ready to serve the lemonade, fill a mason jar with Milky Way Ice cubes and then add lemonade.

CHOCOLATE-PEPPERMINT WAND HOT CHOCOLATE

YIELD: 2 SERVINGS

CHOCOLATE-PEPPERMINT WANDS

¼ cup semisweet chocolate chips

½ teaspoon vegetable shortening

4 peppermint candy sticks

HOT CHOCOLATE

1½ cups heavy cream

1½ cups milk

¼ cup sugar

⅛ teaspoon salt

6 ounces bittersweet chocolate, chopped

3 drops peppermint oil

minimarshmallows, for garnish

To make the Chocolate-Peppermint Wands, line a baking sheet with wax paper.

Combine the semisweet chocolate chips and vegetable shortening together in an uncovered, microwave-safe bowl. Microwave in 20-second intervals on high power, stirring in between, until melted.

Dip one end of each peppermint candy stick in the melted chocolate.

Place the sticks on the prepared baking sheet and refrigerate for 15 minutes or until they are set.

Place white chocolate chips in microwave-safe plastic bag. Microwave in 20-second intervals on medium-high power until melted.

Cut a small corner from the bag. Decorate the chocolate-dipped peppermint sticks with white chocolate drizzle.

Let the sticks stand until they are set. Store them at room temperature.

To make the hot chocolate, in a saucepan, combine the cream, milk, sugar, and salt over medium-low heat.

When the mixture steams, add the chopped chocolate and stir the mixture until the chocolate melts.

Stir in the peppermint oil.

To serve, pour the hot chocolate into the mugs and top it with 1 chocolate-peppermint wand each and minimarshmallows.

Tip: Make it boozy by adding 1½ ounces of your liquor of choice to each mug (Kahlúa, Irish Cream, and so on).

SUNSHINE, DAISIES, BUTTER MELLOW MOCKTAIL

YIELD: 1 SERVING

coconut flakes, for garnish

1½ ounces pineapple juice

½ ounce lime juice

2 to 3 ounces sparkling white grape juice

pineapple leaf, thinly sliced, for garnish (optional)

This yellow cocktail is inspired by a certain failed charm of a rat-owning redhead. Unlike that spell, this fruity mocktail is a near-guaranteed success.

⌣ Pour the coconut flakes onto plate. Wet the rim of the flute and dip the rim into the coconut flakes. Set the flute aside.

⌣ Combine the pineapple and lime juices in a shaker with ice. Shake the juices to combine.

⌣ Strain the drink into the coconut-rimmed flute, and top it with the sparkling grape juice. Garnish with a thinly sliced pineapple leaf, if using.

LAVENDER-LEMON CALMING DRAUGHT

YIELD: 1 SERVING

**LAVENDER
SIMPLE SYRUP**

1 cup water

1 cup white sugar

1 tablespoon fresh
lavender blossoms

**LAVENDER-LEMON
CALMING DRAUGHT
COCKTAIL**

Lavender Simple Syrup

1½ cups freshly squeezed
lemon juice, with pulp

7 cups water

½ cup fresh whole
mint leaves

Lemon slices

Soothing lavender and refreshing lemon combine to make this
calming draught. We will skip the crocodile heart this time.

LAVENDER SIMPLE SYRUP

- To make the Lavender Simple Syrup, combine
  the water, sugar, and lavender blossoms in a small
  saucepan. Bring the mixture to a boil, stirring until
  the sugar dissolves. Simmer the syrup for 1 minute.

- Remove the syrup from the heat and let it steep for
  30 minutes.

- Strain the syrup into a glass jar, seal, and store in
  the refrigerator.

LAVENDER-LEMON CALMING
DRAUGHT COCKTAIL

- To make the calming draught, fill a pitcher with
  ice. Pour the chilled syrup into the pitcher, then
  stir in the lemon juice, 7 cups of water, mint leaves,
  and lemon slices.

- Serve the draught in highball or rocks glasses
  over ice.

> Tip: If you would like to make this potion color
> appropriate, stir into the mixture in the pitcher
> around 5 to 10 drops of blue food coloring and
> then serve the draught.

COLD-CURING
PEPPER CIDER

YIELD: 8 SERVINGS

½ gallon (64 ounces)
apple cider

½ cup Red Hots candies

8 cinnamon sticks, for
garnish (optional)

This Red Hots apple cider is inspired by the classic cold-curing potion. It is best served warm, but you can also chill it overnight and serve it over ice.

- Pour the apple cider and Red Hots candies in a 6-quart pot or Dutch oven.

- Warm over medium heat, stirring the mixture occasionally until the candies have melted and the cider has turned red, around 30 minutes. Do not let the mixture come to a boil.

- Ladle the drink into mugs and add a cinnamon stick as garnish, if using.

> Tip: You do not want the liquid to come to a boil because it will start to reduce. Then you will end up with syrup instead of Pepper-Up Cider!

About the Author

Bertha Barmann is a beverage enthusiast and loves brewing all kinds of potions and elixirs. She lives in Soda Springs, Idaho.